Stalking Joy

Stalking Joy

Margaret Benbow

Texas Tech University Press

The Walt McDonald First-Book Poetry Series

This book was set in Lapidary 333 and Pepita and printed on acid-free paper that meets the guidelines for permanence and durability of the Committee on Production Guidelines for Book Longevity of the Council on Library Resources. ∞

Printed in the United States of America

Book and jacket design by Lisa Camp

Library of Congress Cataloging-in-Publication Data
Benbow, Margaret.
      Stalking joy / Margaret Benbow.
          p.   cm. — (Walt McDonald first-book poetry series)
      ISBN 0-89672-375-5 (acid-free paper)
        I. Title. II. Series.
    PS3552.E5365S83 1997
    811'.54—dc21   96-47109
                                        CIP

97 98 99 00 01 02 03 04 05 06 / 9 8 7 6 5 4 3 2 1

Texas Tech University Press
Box 41037
Lubbock, Texas 79409-1037 USA
1-800-832-4042

Acknowledgments

I am grateful to the editors of the following publication in which a number of my poems, several in earlier versions, first appeared:

Anthology of Magazine Verse and Yearbook of American Poetry, 1981:
   "Silent Star" (originally "The Old Biograph Girl")

Antioch Review: "Woman Carrying Twins"

Audit: "El Gato"

Beloit Poetry Journal: "The Grocer's Daughter"

The Exquisite Corpse: "My Sister and the Bad Review," "Upon Learning My Enemy is Dead"

The Georgia Review: "May and the Misdiagnosis," "The Mother's Night Thoughts"

The Journey Home: "Pheasant," "Tomato Field"

Kenyon Review: "Burlesque Night at Le Cave," "Kala," "Ross's Eyes," "Sauna," "Scarlet Fever"

Madison Review: "Artist: Exhibit A"

Poetry: "Bogeyman," "The Old Biograph Girl," "Hard Freeze," "Out of Hand," "The Queen of Everything," "Racine," "Rose's Farm," "Crazy Arms"

Prairie Schooner: "How to Tell a Bird of Prey," "Interview with Carmela"

Red Weather: "Cat-Burglar," "Punch and Judy," "Trial Separation"

Spoon River Poetry Review: "The Champion," "Jake's Last Proverb," "Rebuke the Devil," "Stalking Joy," "Violencia and the Student"

Wisconsin Academy Review: "Fool for Love," "Hornet and Pear"

In January 1996, Walter McDonald stepped down as editor of the Texas Tech University Press poetry program and the TTUP Poetry Award Series, ending a twenty-year tenure. The Press is indebted to him for his selfless years of service; his unflagging quest for excellence; the truly fine, select list he established in poetry; and, most of all, his friendship. Given his much praised, single-handed, and hands-on management of the TTUP First-Book Poetry competition since 1990, the Press is privileged to announce the naming of the Walt McDonald First-Book Poetry Series.

Though deeply saddened by Walt McDonald's departure, the Press is honored to announce that Robert A. Fink, whose *The Tongues of Men and of Angels* was the first volume to be published in the TTUP Invited Poets Series, has assumed the poetry editorship. The Press looks forward to a long relationship with Robert Fink as he continues the Walt McDonald tradition of asking always, Is this a manuscript that *must* be published? and settling only for one whose excellence answers resoundingly *yes*.

Foreword

In the climactic scene of Bernard Malamud's short story "Idiots First," Mendel—dying, furious that he may have failed to help his son Isaac—lunges for Ginzburg the Angel of Death and begins to choke him. Struggling "nose to nose," Mendel shouts at Ginzburg: "'You bastard, don't you understand what it means human?'" Ginzburg laughs at the absurdity of a "pipsqueak nothing" old Jew trying to strangle Death, but when Ginzburg sees his own reflection in Mendel's eyes—"a shimmering, starry, blinding light that produced darkness,"—dumbfounded, he replies, "'Who, me?'" and grants Mendel the additional minutes necessary to provide for his son. Having done so, the train departing with Isaac safely aboard, Mendel turns back and ascends the stairs "to see what had become of Ginzburg." Mendel has forced the Angel of Death to recognize that he, not Mendel, is the "pipsqueak nothing," since Ginzburg can only kill, not create, not love, not sacrifice, not suffer, not forgive. Mendel has dared to confront Ginzburg with "what it means human." Poets know this confrontation with the human makes us vulnerable. Poet and reader must dare to see, hear, touch, taste, and smell. Great poetry is physical, and readers who climb through the ropes into the ring of shared experience can expect to come away sweaty and stinging. And joyful.

How fitting that Margaret Benbow's book is entitled *Stalking Joy.* Stalking joy is exactly what Walt McDonald has been doing through-out his life, his poetry, and his tenure as the first poetry editor of Texas Tech University Press. Walt has found particular joy discover-ing through his reading of literary journals poets whose work reveals what it means human. Margaret Benbow is the sixth poet whose manuscript Walt McDonald has selected for publication in TTUP's First-Book Poetry Series. Each of these books—Cathy Smith Bowers's *The Love That Ended Yesterday In Texas,* Laurie Kutchins's *Between Towns,* Shelly Wagner's *The Andrew Poems,* Deborah Burn-ham's *Anna and the Steel Mill,* Laura Fargas's *An Animal of the Sixth Day,* and Margaret Benbow's *Stalking Joy*—celebrates family, faith, the land and its people, unconditional love, earned joy. These are values Walt McDonald holds dear. Walt has been my good friend for twenty-four years. His fifteen published collections of poetry (garnering such awards as the Juniper Prize and the George Elliston Prize, three National Cowboy Hall of Fame Western Heritage Awards and three Poetry Prizes from the Texas Institute of Letters) and his more than fifteen hundred poems published in journals testify to Walt's devotion to writing lasting poetry. His poems have instructed me in poetic craft and immersed me in the beauty of language, but even more importantly, Walt's poems insist that being human means we are responsible for each other. There are no islands in Walt McDonald's world: "We're not alone. / When we drive flat roads to town, / neighbors miles away look up and wave" ("Neighbors Miles Away" from *Counting Survivors*).

This theology is reflected in Walt's work as poetry editor. Referring to Shelly Wagner in the preface to her poetry collection *The Andrew Poems,* Walt states, "This woman has looked into her heart and written with grace, without flinching." Such courage and grace also reflect Walt McDonald's approach to writing poetry and to selecting manuscripts for the TTUP First-Book Poetry Series. This past January, Walt decided to step down as poetry editor. The Press reluctantly accepted his resignation, and as a fitting tribute to Walt's devotion, rechristened the series for him.

It is especially appropriate that Margaret Benbow's vibrant, life-singing book *Stalking Joy* should be Walt's final selection. I'm certain Walt was immediately taken by the title. It is almost a poem in itself: imagistic, metaphorical, energetic, complex in its connotations, and thematic. The title prepares the reader for a quest, not for fickle *happiness,* whose pursuit is unworthy, but *joy,* more durable and much harder won.

The book's epigraph from Flannery O'Connor—"Picture me with my ground teeth stalking joy"—declares the personae will be dogged in their pursuit. The poem "Fatemark" may best reflect the tone of this quest and the thematic motif of the book: an individual comes into life with "the nerve" and "the blood" and sets off after joy "at a breakneck breakheart pace, now and ever / hothead first." The only instruction given is: *"live or else,"* both a warning and a threat. "You're marked for life / with the good and ill of what you are." The challenge to pursue a life of passion and commitment is not unlike Henry David Thoreau's famous declaration in *Walden:* "I went to the woods because I wished to live deliberately, to front only the essential facts of life, and see if I could not learn what it had to teach, and not, when I came to die, discover that I had not lived."

Stalking Joy's five sections orchestrate the quest for joy, introducing in "Root of the Ear: the Neighborhood" a world of sexuality, "hissed insults," and "robbers," enough to give the child-persona of "Racine" nightmares. "Grandpa" is her protector, armed with shotgun, Bowie knife and "old Boche rifle with fixed bayonet." In "Kala," Avery, the "four-eyed / youngest son of the fairy tale," finds his saviors in books, specifically Kala, Tarzan's ape mother: *"he feels the heavy charms of her arms."* Children need champions, joy coming with the arrival of their heroes, but when children grow up, they may find joy elusive.

The people of Margaret Benbow's neighborhood are out to corner joy. They seek it in passion—the lust for flesh, a paradox of pleasure and pain: "How happy I was, in his clutches!" "I kissed him so hard my nose bled" ("Crazy Arms: Earlene Remembers"). "Madame de Stael bragged about the gymnastic lover / who dragged her by her hair from attic to cellar" ("Violencia and the Student"). Carmela ("Interview with Carmela") "had the nerve"; she "was the girl in the circus / who puts her head in the lion's mouth." Her smile was "hot and bright enough / to break all the lion's teeth." The bogeyman in a girl's dreams is "a beautiful young man, romantically pale" ("Bogeyman"). He is "an angel-haired / sexy prince, giving off heat and light / like a blast furnace." He is more dangerous than the "robbers" in the child's dream in "Racine." When the girl cries out in the night and her "cleanneck aunts / swarm into the room, case the corners," the girl finds no ease in this rescue. Joy is to be found with her demon lover, but *she* is the one doing the pursuing, the one to be reckoned with as she whispers at the "spangled glass" of "the tight window": *"I will kill you / if you don't come back.*" This is a tough neighborhood where women like May ("May and the Misdiagnosis: Fighting Back") refuse their "turn for a wasting disease," defying Death—"the old skull" —and his minion doctors. Even when Death wins—exploding Andreas ("Larson Arson") "through the wall like a knife, / every pore, tooth, and hair burned clear," the death scene is classic Hollywood: *"Is everybody toasty?"* What the citizens of this neighborhood fear is not *dying,* but never having lived. They choose joy and follow God's dictate: *"Take what you want, and pay for it"* ("Jake's Last Proverb"). Death for them means being only an observer (a reader, a writer): "I myself touched nothing but paper. / Nothing" ("Violencia and the Student"). They want to be swept away by "damburst angels," not condemned to go home and commit "extensive notes" to "narcissus-white paper."

Having established the motifs in the book's first section, Benbow develops in the middle three sections—"The Hot Theatre of the Head," "Lessons of the Flesh," and "The Raptor's Eye"—the lust for joy. Most of these personae are women. They speak of the pain and loss that accompanies their life quest. Old age and breakups make the personae more cynical about the pursuit of joy, but they do not forget—"my face once glowed in the dark" ("Silent Star")—or deny their passion; each remains like Aunt Lucrece ("Laura's Visit to Aunt Lucrece") "a howling mammal . . . / with nostrils flaring like spores." Even if they take Christ as their lover, the joy he brings is sensual, not spiritual: "he rubs his beard / over every scar of needle or knife, / wound patterns deep as bone" ("Rebuke the Devil"). These women know the risks of passion—its violence, the "Punch and Judy" show. They hear the "heart murmur, / *let me fly by night*" ("Hard Freeze for Lyn and Barry"). Joy is more compelling than the voice cautioning restraint, so they give "a big bad kiss, . . . / aim for the heart, make things jump" ("Out of Hand"). Each fears being alone downstairs while upstairs, Rapunzel and her cat-burglar lover are "hoofing it / like a roomful of drunken shakers" ("Cat-Burglar"). None wants to taste that "instant's sad bile as she realizes / how entirely she is out of danger."

The final section, "Memory Jug," recapitulates the book's thematic motifs, but rather than ending the quest and resolving the paradoxes, the personae celebrate the process: here is the map to joy; yes, let us continue; let us begin again. The last image in the book suggests new beginnings, new adventures: the young girl, now back among the living after almost dying from scarlet fever looks out the window at a rose, "lips / pressed against the glass, archipelagoes of leaves / flying into the dark" ("Scarlet Fever").

The principal focus of this section is family, especially mothers and sisters—sources of encouragement and salvation. A daughter thinks she will find joy by breaking out of the "hive of the family," even though it "provided abundance of sweet" ("Stalking Joy"). The daughter feels suffocated in the family cave: "The young, like murder, like art, will out / in the most surprising places." A young mother recognizes her source of joy to be her newborn child: "I'd spot you / and sit beside you, ticking with love, purple heart / on sleeve" ("Ross's Eyes"). Another mother tries to save her son: "I pounced for his curls / and braided him tight to earth" ("Prodigal and Mother"). In "Rose's Farm," Rose mothers a young woman: Rose "was glad to see me; / she swaddled me in afghans / smelling of all her favorite dogs." In "Scarlet Fever," the young daughter is drowning in fever: *Mama* / I cried again. And a hand / wound itself in my hank of hair and lifted me" ("Scarlet Fever"). These women are joy-givers, life-bringers: Mother Nature Rose cooks "a big fat chicken / coughing with sweet paprika" and sets the dish before her son Roy—"a hammer man at the [Chicago] stockyards" ("Rose's Farm"), then traps between her knees "a little hog torn by a dog." She throws the "screaming trotter" on its side, stuffs the "guts back into their hole" and sews up the wound "with needle and strong twine." The mother in "Scarlet Fever" rescues her daughter from the delirium of black-bomber fish, undersea monsters reeling after the child "with hagfish screams and groans." The daughter is snapped into light "stone gold": "My mother was combing / my lunatic mane." One persona's sister ("The Bad Review and My Sister") is a mother "whose back is like a little wall / and whose children haul themselves up on her braids / hand over hand." She plants her heel on a reviewer-serpent's head, rescuing her poet sister from self-doubt and despair when the reviewer hisses that all who hear the persona's poems will "puke." Sister-God threatens the serpent: "where I come from / people make wallets out of snakes."

The mood of this world-neighborhood remains "one of hazard" ("Pheasant") where the quest for joy is bonded to the lust for flesh—the "tawny heart thaws and turns, / hums with the season"—beauty and pain: "articulated beak and copper claw." In "The Philosophy Major's Hair," a smitten coed declares, "I could have clipped topiary shapes of Adam and Eve, / their fast-breeding menagerie and garden of delight." For the persona of "Fool for Love," there will be no sedate old age. When she is "an old burning loaf of a woman," she will "look into the eyes of some hairy attendant" who makes her bed, counts her bones, and answer his questions "'Are you comfortable?' . . . 'What more can I do?'" by giving him a *film noir look and hiss, / 'Mon Dieu, are you not man enough to know? / Read my lips.'"*

For Mendel, for Margaret Benbow, for Walt McDonald, for the personae of *Stalking Joy,* being *human* means grappling with the Angels of Life and Death in whatever protean forms they take: Ginzburg, scarlet fever, prodigal children, the woodsman lover smelling of "creosote and raw furs" ("Hornet and Pear"). The denizens of Margaret Benbow's world will settle for nothing less than joy. They will *live or else.*

Robert A. Fink
Editor
Walt McDonald First-Book Poetry Series

Contents

To my family

Picture me with my ground teeth stalking joy.
Flannery O'Connor

Root
of the Ear:
the *Neighborhood*

Racine

Days we walked to Oscar's store. It was dark,
and crammed with food whose smells and names
my grandfather liked: blutwurst, clabber.
There were black boulders of loaves, and violet
twigs of deep-sea fishes dried to lace.
Oscar gave me candy, or blackjack gum. We talked.

Across the street, "old fool Sorris's" bold young bride,
stripped to the sweetbreads, lay athwart a hammock
in her Sheena jungle clout and read comics,
lips moving, or stretched out her long legs
water-colored and pink and absently prodded the belly
and saffron heart of Riki, her yappy Peke.
Sorris would poke his angry spud of a face
around the screen door: just checking.
He and my grandfather, enemies from boyhood, hissed insults
and sneered behind smelly stogies. "Soreass!" jeered Grandpa,
and of the luxury dog Riki, "Ratbait!"
Then we walked slowly home,
and he told my mother I'd been good.
She hugged me, and I got to wear
her rose-quartz star in my hair.

Spring days were plumed with pink lilac, but one midnight
black as hell I woke bolt upright and *knew*
I'd heard them: the robbers, who would
get me first. Hot tears, cold sweat.
Oh, I wept and prayed to Jesus and God
and to "GRANDMA! GRANDMA!" that blue-eyed

English angel. Grandpa heard me,
stumped up grumping: he'd like to see the bastards *try* it.
He showed me his shotgun, his Bowie knife
and an old Boche rifle with fixed bayonet.
I sobbed with relief, then smiled,
then slept. Beneath lilac
robbers croaked, yards deep.

Kala

SLAM, stepfather's home. THUMP,
commando boots hit the corner. BELCH,
stew time. Mom dumps
bomb-sized meatballs on his plate. He
shoves them into his food hole.

In the bedroom, Avery the reader, the four-eyed
youngest son of the fairy tale, closes
Tarzan of the Apes in a panic,
rushes to the table. ROAR, BRAY,
he's late. Tears drizzle
into his alphabet soup, sog up the dumplings:
but he sees his mother's coat, that tumult of foxes
rushing sleek and apricot from its hanger. In the corner
lie the guinea pig and her pups, witless boobies
tugging at the pink stars on her belly.
If he, like Tarzan,
had an ape mother named Kala—

and he feels the heavy charms of her arms.
She lifts him to her back.
They emerge into full sun. Crotons
push their orange and red faces against him.
What radiant heat.

Kala can't read, but she is kind.
She protects him from bad cats in the jungle
and monsters knobbed like a brass bedstead.
She carries him piggyback,
peewee, hairless though he is, and when it rains
they stay monkey-balled in a tree

and watch the storm.
She rubs her face
against the damp blossoms of his cheek and neck.
Just once

she takes him to the clearing, the cabin
where his parents died. Lady Greystoke
was crazy as well as castaway. Here are some little
daisy-stem bones, and a tatter of lilac lawn.
The cabin is leached white. Every object seems sunstruck.
Avery backs away,
holds out the blond pips of his arms to Kala.
She takes them in her great hands
and holds him against the turbine of her heart.
They go outside. The plantain lilies blow.
They watch the twilight come down, animal brown.

Crazy Arms: Earlene Remembers

Though I grew up to marry a snowman,
though I look like a glass of milk,

once I was the queen of consuming passions:
and in my mind distant hotbeds
buck and bloom with big-bear hugs, pink
tulip skin, and the edible wild plants
of lips and ears. Oh, Dave may have been
just a lord of the streets,
but he was Baby Child to me.
He would rub his harsh curls
against my neck, and tug with excellent teeth
at the peach chemise made for big tomatoes.
I breathed beastly suggestions
in his marvelously ready ear . . .
How happy I was, in his clutches!
Words failed us, we fell into broken English
and then to the searing nubs of vowels,
Ahh, ee, I, ohh, you.

A night lush with stars.
"Look at me, baby."
I kissed him so hard my nose bled,
and he said: "Welcome to rock and roll."

Jake's Last Proverb

Some of Jake's proverbs tasted sweet,
torn from chunks of halvah,
but his favorites were hardened in immigrant lye
and slammed down like bricks:
Revenge is a dish best served cold.
The main thing is to outlive the bastards.
Everything inside a dragon is red, meaning
monsters exist, gut full of evil.

Jake despised the stunted lives
of those who'd ignored his advice. They were
pumpkin-assed layabouts, cowbirds and screwups,
crushing their father's birdy shoulders,
hanging about their mother's neck like goiters.
Some were in jail, others dead,
smelling up a world of hurt. *Forward over graves,*
Jake counseled the parents, waving away
their smashed bad eggs.

Jake died. One day I passed his shop
and suddenly a turn of light showed ghosts and angels
mouthing in the glass.
Their lips stuttered in a lurid palsy
of advice and malediction, stinking clinkers
of demented truisms, sachets of epigrams
and sea stones of proverbs,
clear as a saint's ancient deadeye.
When all was said and done
there were only ten words, inevitable,
massive as the big bones of the strongest animal:

Take what you want, and pay for it, says God.

Then silence, and the wind filling with white hair.

The Champion

Therese likes Dominick best of the bullet boys.
He's huge, her kind of devil, bombing around
in terrifying bloodguilt-black clothes

but Dominick's mother can't stand Therese
and when one night she sees them cleated together

her teeth grow long as a fork
she bolts outside, disaster in her hair,

to ram coals of counsel in his ear,
to make the girl suffer
for walking that walk. Under the lotus stars
she brains them with humps and thighbones
and snaggle teeth of Calabrian curse words,
snarls in Therese's hair like a fruit bat,
garrotes Dominick's neck with thumb bruises,
bounces him off walls, thumps her breast
and announces to the neighbors in a pitiful voice
he is killing me. She flays and enlaces her bison son
with mother tongue, sorts out his complex of limbs
and refrigerator-walks him home. At their doorstep
she says *You have no idea what I would do for you,
solo tu,* for you alone.

El Gato: **Underground**

He's got blue beads against snakebite,
white beads against drought,
a knife for bad-eyed skinheads
and boots for the killing floor.
He's protected: warnings are
slipped through the door with the milk,
he's perfected two-way mirrors
that will catch the reds of their eyes
before they catch his.
It's symmetrical, it should work

except for the spark in the stable:
any crazy mule
can jump ahead of a kindly rumor,
bumble jack-assed through your mirrors,
stand before you on four fat hooves
and bray a motto for your sampler
that would change the shape of your ear.

The Grocer's Daughter

He asked for pâte, then watched
while she painted the black eye of a truffle
with pimento pupils, rays of almond lashes.
(Her own eyes were Java brown.)
Then she took a hunk of brawn from a platter
and while he breathed on the display case,
sank her teeth in it.
His heart fell gasping in the pickle barrel,
resurfaced rich and strange. He floated out on clouds of dill.
Called later, she would, and did, go with him to a movie,
a restaurant, home to drink wine, and then, just before
his painfully bided time ran out, to the sheets
he'd been frantically preparing for a week.
The girl was a gold medalist,
a queen of the roman rings: he could barely hold on
with both arms and both legs.
(She'd been divorced three times, and neighborhood gossip
hung a string of garlicky adulteries about her neck).

Pressed, she moved in, bringing a side of beef—rose-red loin,
tender enough to cut with a tongue—and her half-caste
Siamese cats. They pigged down odds and ends of shellfish,
then dotted the apartment
with exotic green droppings, florid puke. She too
ate her head off, soaked in the tub for hours,
had many messy little ways.
But she baked bread, and for him
the sourdough bubbled with hallucinogens.
He took her to the park, and she, who'd seen
a Mafioso gunned in two
a dozen feet from the fish counter
walked with one hand on his neck

ready to jump into a tree
at the first sign of a chipmunk foaming at the mouth.
She was the only woman he'd ever known who, after a bath,
would hang around for hours forgetting to dress.
When she did, her little eyelet camisole
twanged him like catgut.

After a month she left, telling him
that because of the holiday coming up
everything was going great guns at the shop
and they needed her at all hours, making Easter
pigeon bread, sticking rosemary into lambs.

He'd bought some new towels, suspiciously cheap,
and the night before she left
he saw her in the bathroom, rubbing down, stark-
staring back at him with savage red breast and haunches.

When she left, a few things stayed.
There was a saucer of darkening chicken hearts,
meant for the cats' nervous stomachs.
The washer suddenly began to go screwy,
shaking and banging its head against the wall.
A workman's horny hand probed deep into the works, fished out
the tag-end of a shredded bra.

He called his old Army friend John, and John said:
What you need, Son, is to get *laid*.

He hung up, decided to have supper. One last
yard-long black hair
turned up in the soup.

Violencia and the Student

That fall I read like crazy.
In my rat brown garret, Heathcliff's red breath
burned Cathy to ash. *Haunt me,* he said, *drive me mad.*
Elsewhere
Madame de Stael bragged about the gymnastic lover
who dragged her by her hair from attic to cellar,
she kicked his aristo butt all around the boudoir.
I myself touched nothing but paper.
Nothing.

In the room below, Marie had a fight with Scott.
She slapped his head off, he stormed out.
She threw his stereo out the window, in her comet heels
and red star dress she chased his motorcycle
through midnight traffic, she wrote
SCOTT DOES DOGS on the wall of his favorite bar.
Then she came home and began to suffer.
She couldn't eat, couldn't sleep,
wrapped his scarf around her neck in a tight choker,
seared her arms with red love letters,
cried and prayed, flirted with *santeria* (her little cat
disappeared), bought jinx-remover powder,
drank until she dropped,
crawled to bed.

That night Marie awoke
to see rivers of angels;
they rose and fell all night. Marie's joyous screams
bounced neighbors out of bed,
Scott's Harley roared at the curb. Anointed with miracle
she showed herself at the window, discreetly veiled, praying.
Her lace mantilla, her damburst angels

inflamed Scott's intentions. Their white wedding followed,
and as best friend I led the toasts.
Then I went home and, to narcissus-white paper,
committed extensive notes.

May and the Misdiagnosis: Fighting Back

One day the doctor told May
your turn for a wasting disease,
but she refused to let him
prop her ribcage up a tree just yet.
Instead, she began eating her head off.
She lived on lard, all her nerve endings
sheathed in rosy fat.
She dunked her rosette curls
into butter tubs of gluttony.
She spit on her bad gut, her bad heart,
and all but the most sumptuous
deadly sins.
The doomy wag of the doctor's tongue
had twisted her to the roots, but
closer to the earth
she prized up gobs of tubers, anklets of peanuts,
and embraced whole racks of lamb.
She saw the doctor chop bits most cherished
from other patients. Savagely physicked,
they crawled to the cooling board.
May ate steadily forward,
never putting a foot wrong,
gilding every jiggle, dimple and crease.
On appointment days the doctor would look at her,
sitting on two chairs, her big smile
smelling of pie and ham fat,
and the old skull would fall silent.

Woman Carrying Twins

Mornings I sprawl in my bath like a big Susannah
while under my ribcage goggle-eyed children
head downward through water of nautilus green.
Robed in white and sitting down to the breakfast farina,
I'm a skintight madonna, full of fat chances,
with the gravid bloom of a still life's plums.

But the blood brothers wake to find themselves
locked drumstick limb to limb: and they fight
like tigers in a bag,
to mark what turf they're heir to. Red-hot,
their bloodlines tangle
in tugs of war too fast to follow. Barging around
under my skin, they drive each other
hog-wild.

Hours later I sip milk, sit still, listen: one dwarf heel
still beats time, the other drums blood through
my giantess heart.

Interview with Carmela

This old babe in gunmetal mink
had a snootful before we met. Her red-hot mama
true confessions crank up and overflow
on breath purple with grappa:
old rich baboons, blue-faced financiers
who pursued her fifty years before, and Bugsy Siegel,
that cheap hood: this firework, work of fire,
heaves and reddens at the memory
of gems too small. Why, "Boiling Jam"
was written for Carmela, everyone in the band
knew her name. I've heard it all before,
and as I smooth the tame flanks of my gray suit,
I know it's true. Mafia boy bandit kings
used to crawl up
and beg her to stand on their hearts
with stiletto heels. She still has
as illiterate note from Warren Harding;
she called him Uncle Sugar. In his loopy backhand
she will always be "terrible beautiful"
and drive him "crazy wild,"
a sort of Josephine (to whom Napoleon wrote,
I'll be home in two days. Don't bathe.)

"Legs took my hand
and licked my fingers, every one. Oh yeah:
I had the nerve,
I was the girl in the circus
who puts her head in the lion's mouth.
And you know what?
He trembled. Not me."
Her lips gleam with cream,
her tongue is a noble purple,
and her smile hot and bright enough
to break all the lion's teeth.

Larson Arson

Andreas and Carl Larson were the thug twins.
They lit up the wolf at the door,
burned things down.

We would see them in night cars, Andreas so handsome
we called him the ace of face, and Carl
with a thousand dollars of black leather
running over his body
like the tender hands of his girl.
We booked their doom, called them
silver skeletons riding, were surprised
they burned and burned, and lived to tell.

Larson Arson was on the job
when Andreas saw the gas jet and Carl didn't
and had just time to torch the rags and grin and say
Is everybody toasty?
when Andreas was blown through the wall like a knife,
every pore, tooth, and hair burned clear;
every bone in his body broken;
not enough left to bury.
Carl was thrown through an open window
into the thickest flowering bush in town.
He stepped down as though from his mother's palm
and walked past his molten double
without missing stride.

Carl gave up fire. He said he didn't
want to die roasting like a pig in hell.
People love human brands
snatched from the burning, and from that day

Carl was the darling wherever he went.
Roads smoothed themselves before him,
landscapes bloomed before their time.
Old rooms of fire
gilded his new skin of reformation.
Old rooms of smoke, those thumbs on the throat,
were glamorous sandalwood at the banquet.

Bogeyman

He was out there running crazy
with his red-hot bulgy eyes rolling around
looking for dirty greedy crabby little girls
like me, oh, just like me.
I lay stark awake, sweating bullets,
afraid to look at the window:
surely I would see his wolf-snout,
his bawdy red tongue mashed against the glass.

One night he did come, and stood
at the foot of the bed
while I stared and stared.
He was a beautiful young man, romantically pale—
and what a mouth, what eyes!
When he smiled, what choppers,
white as snow! (Was he
mad, bad, and dangerous to know?) I'd expected
horns: and that he'd gibber, and bounce off walls
like an ape. Yet here he was, an angel-haired
sexy prince, giving off heat and light
like a blast furnace.
He whispered:
"Rise and shine, little queenie.
Come to Bogey, do."
His tongue, that red snapper, flicked
between his lips, and he stood
making loverboy eyes at me.
I thought *Trouble trouble trouble*
and I said "No no no!"
He leaned closer, so that I could feel
the hot corona of his curls,

and spoke in a voice
of burnt-black sugar:
"My lost Rosetta, my little stolen Ruby . . .
you expected a monster mauler, you thought
that somewhere there simmered jiggly
tutti-fruttis into which I chopped my pets.
Yet here I am, mild as mother's milk.
Here is my kiss, of pulsing silk!"
He paused, then added in businesslike tones,
"I wish, shortcake, you'd open your eyes
and then you'd see
my big surprise."

Hard gold lamplight, screams:
my cleanneck aunts
swarm into the room, case the corners—
but I'm alone. "Nightmares," they explain,
"too much pepperbelly food,"
and show me the tight window,
and night pure as a bunny: nothing out there
but dippers of stars.

What then do they make of me
kneeling and putting my lips to the spangled glass
and breathing blood red from the heart

I will kill you
if you don't come back.

The
Hot
Theatre
of the
Head

Silent Star

Not even the angels could bring a breath of air
to a white-hot day in Los Angeles.
A blue jay sits in the lemon tree, surrounded by
half-painted Easter eggs. He's
dead calm: a still life, you see.

In the photo, that's me,
my bound black hair and silk lashes
bent beneath the engorged gaze of—Walter Long?
One of the Beery's? Anyhow, "a human pig," rooting toward me
with sag belly and straining braces, bent on playing
his hot customary part. But the humid human hand
never touched this star. (Ramon Novarro
rescued me. I wept. He kissed my hem.) And at premieres
I was the orchid lady in the black sedan,
and Mother the earthy turnip
stumping at my side. As for money—
never mind: I noticed in time the dictionary truth
that *star turn* is next to *starvation,*
but just a little way from *stash.*
I'm sitting pretty on mounds of nest eggs.
The one thing I could use, like the blue jay,
like that girl

running along the beach in her sandy maillot,
is some relief
from the blood heat of the day. La Belle Otero died
between one bite of rabbit stew
and the next, under a sky of crockery blue. All of us,

the bird, each leaf of the jacaranda tree, my rouged lips
exhale the same parched scrap of dialogue: *send rain.*
I address at last
a browbeating golden hairy lover, and I remember
how coolly
my face once glowed in the dark.

The Mother's Night Thoughts

I know I must remain calm

but the house that stood in soft vegetable peace
now smokes with chaos, a boy
sweaty, snarly, and lewd
lays the fleshy folds of his lips on my daughter
and I want to say to her
Baby, don't give him your high temperature,
don't give him your sugar,

because he knows nothing of my girl, her radiant strangeness.

I see her walk her goddess walk
while he snorts and bellows after,
his liver and his muffler hanging by a thread.
In the hot theater of the head
mothers from revenge westerns and murder ballads
ride horses to death to save my lily daughter,
slip knives between his fat
short ribs and rear up in old bloody matriarch curses:
May his tongue and loins be struck by lightning!

Dawn turns my nightdress diablo red
while schemes coil and heave in my brain of knots,

how to make my blue baby cough up loverboy,
how to turn this cad into road kill,
how to, oh Christ,
burn him down and kiss him good-bye.

Artist: Exhibit A

I do not know love. To say "I love you"
would break all my teeth.
                                    Paul Gauguin

This year you're famous. Last year you were only
infamous, and night after night
your trueblood painter's girl Maidy
would scrub you like a pot.
She hid your knives, dumped your stash,
and in time
she became the light of your red-salt eyes.
You painted a radiant woman gliding upward
through the darkest of waves,
water pearls flowing from shoulders like wings.

The privileges of art are enormous,
and today we've come to admire you,
still tasting the morning's review:
"His paintings are like the thoughts
that might go through an attack dog's head
after a heavy night on the circuits."
Then, too, there are private rumors
about your mind: "Strictly
brains in black butter, my dear."

You embrace me as someone
who knew you when.
You'll forgive me for saying
you smell so good I hardly recognize you.
Covertly I study your eye-holes: baby clear, nothing there

to suggest what I'd heard. You look saved.
With gentle gestures you guide me
toward your pride, the new portrait of Maidy.

Maidy living has the forehead of a good child,
and cub's hair, full of curls and sparks. In the picture
hag spirals explode from her skull to cyclone
points of the globe. Her forehead is smeared with antimony,
lips split like a melon spraying teeth seeds,
ribcage sprung.
She is a house hit by a fireball.
"Darkly thrilling," breathes someone behind me.

I look at you, and you smile modestly.
Maidy stands beside you in her robin's-egg blue shirt, that hair
simmering around her face. Her eyes tell me
that is not the way I am
and I think

yet,
poor baby egg.
Yet.

Laura's Visit to Aunt Lucrece

Laura:
>　"Wicked old," whispered my mother, and "Drugs,"
>　and something about *"a male companion . . .*
>　he calls himself a poet, but I'm sure
>　she keeps him around for *you-know-what."*
>　"Nonsense," said my father, "fool gossip.
>　Lucrece just loves young people.
>　So nice of her to arrange
>　a snug little slumber party for Laura . . .
>　cocoa, cinnamon toast . . . the Late Show.
>　Don't be an old hen. Let the girl go!"

　　* * *

The Male Companion:
>　Midnight, and the old lady
>　had long since hit the hay. The house rocked
>　in a whale's belly of a storm. Laura and I
>　crept through the passage vibrating like goblets,
>　out the door and into the lily garden.
>　The flowers staggered, beset,
>　but still they bloomed like a house afire,
>　and she ran around in her nightie
>　with the millipedes, and with every creepy-crawly
>　while the storm destroyed the stars.
>　Just a sound, a moan from the gardener's shed
>　and we turned to see to see to see

>　a howling mammal *something* in a long pale robe
>　with nostrils flaring like spores
>　and each petal of the great cut
>　flower of her head
>　stark white, and rayed with rain.
>　The creature stood on its hind legs

and took in Laura's wringing mermaid gown, the pink fish
of her breast. It stumbled toward us arms out
and became suddenly
the old bag reeking of grappa.
Oh, Laura seized my hand and cried out.
The old woman fell back, mashed her paw to her mouth,
and sped away on molting mules.

Rebuke the Devil

The talented folk artist Sister Morgan was also a religious fanatic.
In the 1950s, her obsession with Christ deepened. She began wearing only white
clothing in preparation for her marriage to him.

You must understand that in my youth
I knew no better
that I found a deep heavy comfort
in the pig-pile of the world
lived in a red cave
of sugar and sex and blues harps
and loved the dear meat, the sweet meat
of the human man

never knew each sin was a meteor
smaller than a grape
lodged like a bullet in the rickrack spine

but then at the meeting Brother Jim
was touched with a Christly gold
brand upon the tongue and he cried
    Oh you foul abundance of evil woman
    you're just a mess of crunchy bones
    to the devil,
    you aren't Queen Morgan to him.
    Aren't you ashamed to wear
    those breeding colors?
    Don't you know you are
    God's tiny child?
    You are in terrible trouble.
    Change that stinking rag of your life.
    Stop eating pig! Stop ratting your hair!

Oh my life, bricked up by sin on sin.
I thought, he is right.

Then I thought
No. I'm not damned just because Jim says so.
Let my hair fill the cave until it explodes.
My star may be drunk, but it can blast heavenward
and I'll see my young love eye to eye.
Around him will be big bodyguard angels
but he will be biggest of all
and dressed in white like me

I'll stand before him in maiden silk
white as madonna lilies
light as a milkweed pod
and I'll say what I've never said to any man

then the big angels will cry "Shame
shame shame!" and grab to bind. Their arms,
they paralyze. *Fear not,* my Jesus says,
and the iron links of angel arms
fall like grass. I hide my face
in his loving white shirt and he says
*Never mind them. We're all
big-star bound.*

What thick hair he has, the lion's
thundercloud of fur.
He suffers my caress.
Then he rubs his beard
over every scar of needle or knife,
wound patterns deep as bone,
and every place I feel his curls
the skin grows new and fine.

Tomato Field

Sun beams fall like stones. Glazed
neck and neck we stump down the rows,
and when we dig in, each spade full, pure clay,
has us jumping up and down. Over the fence,
cows gander, udders boggling against
broad beans and trilliums. They look dimly pleased,
as though at the turn things have taken in some
cool green fourth stomach.

But we madden by degrees.
First we wilt, endangered flora, but by noon
a beef-jerky man and woman shovel and hiss.
You're brown as an ape man, your hair going berserk.
The children rush out, seize my knees. Mama
nuzzles these baby carrots with her
horse lips.

High noon! oh, ready to cry fire I remember
the storm going straight down, no time
between crash and flash. Here
red lanterns of tomatoes
sizzle on straw. I take a hot mouthful
into my hot mouth, lose breath: a kiss
gullet-deep, equatorial.

Executive Secretary: Eileen's Revenge

Think like a revolutionary, live like a bourgeois.
                            Gustave Flaubert

Man's fur lies beneath a white shirt.
My boss is fat on the money pasture.
I picture him high king over all the rest,
a pharaoh bull grazing naked on our fields all day.
Is he a bull, or a whale of a car?
I plot how to shove my dreams in his exhaust pipe,
how to light him up.

Revenge is a dish best served cold.
My pharaoh thinks his workers
are smooth little chanterelles in the corporate ragout.
It's true there are human mushrooms for every use,
but mistaken identities can turn you mold blue, have you
heaving up your life. Pharaoh doesn't know
which of us glow in the dark, which kill the host.

Options nestle their iridescent fuses close to hand.
I don't know how or when, but I know who.

35

The Queen of Everything

Lily ignites old portraits,
her head set in light flammable laces
under a floradora hat. On each side
are her sisters, adorned with the names of
pet dogs and opera creams: May Belle, Annaclair.
Their bodies rear in convulsions of ruffles,
cream-puff bosoms
swelled up by charming corsetry. On each mouth
is a smile in which butter wouldn't melt.
Yet their eyes gleam
trigger-happy, bituminous:
weird little infantas, named
The Wild or The Cruel.

Lily married, and then grew mad as a hornet.
She went crazy rapidly, like a house afire,
or a strong young runner storming the goal.
Her husband confined her to the asylum with tears
and within six months he suffered breakdowns, blackouts.
But Lily loved her new home.
She thrived in her lunatic's shift of unbleached muslin
and waxed fat and fragrant, an immense cabbage rose
flinging seed and scent. Her hair sprang forth
with criminal vitality, the skin of her face and neck
bloomed tenderly, a baby nectarine.
 "I am Maia," she declared proudly to visitors,
and to the doctors who spoke of her condition,
she replied with contempt, "Rooty toot toot!"

Meanwhile, her husband drooped around
and grew yellow as a duck's bill.
He succumbed to a typhoid
of raging proportions. Even in his delirium
he saw Lily approaching, her hair fine and red

under a widow's mantilla of black lace.
Her eyes were the green of limes and kiwis,
and they smiled so kindly. He held out
the ten bleached twigs of his fingers,
and she seized them warmly.
Then she told him what he'd waited to hear.
She forgave him, she said,
for having had his wicked will of her
when she was nineteen, an unprotected female
and a new bride. It had been a terrible shock,
but she forgave him.
Then she put her arms around his little shaven head
and hugged him to her, and they both wept.

Lessons
of the
Flesh

Out of Hand

Look at his eyes,
how they hypnotize.

After midnight, and thanks to you,
a loving mama is out too late at night.
Wildlife shimmers through turquoise rain:
three blondes pale as radium
rise and shine, jump and shout
before their man, dark and dangerous
Mr. W.H.A.M. Did you ever see
wild women tango
past flowers that smell like hot jam?

Even the cats, little twisters,
are up to something
animal fast in the lemon grass.

Oh, back in baby's arms
feeling runs high. "Prove it!" you hiss.
In the red-hot rainy darkness, I
give you a big bad kiss, and we
aim for the heart, make things jump.

Hornet and Pear

They walk as far as the shattered tree
with its single pear. He names things for her
bold as Adam: foxtail millet, Spanish grass.
Nightfall, never fail, catches them
without a stitch between them, as the birds circle home
to light. His kiss cleats to her lip: and she notices
his woodsman's smell of creosote and raw furs.
Heart set, and three months gone, she ignores
the symbols prodding at her ribs: that hornet
staggering away, too gorged to fly, from the pear
gone leadbelly grey around its neat drill holes
and the white fox skin nailed to the shed door.

Sauna

That winter your rich babe
joined the health club. In saunas, she and I
sweated and stewed, and dryly
sized each other up. Steam blue as gentians
swirled between our dirty looks.
My birthmark, my cesarean scar
marked the hide of a sturdy prole, built to last,
and I came only as high as her surly heart.
She thought to herself: *peasant, shorty,*
mother of chubby babies. But the hamstrings stood out
in her hunter's legs. Her skin was all fired up
from a decade of gutsy martinis. Her nose flipped,
a miracle, a little crown princess of rhinoplasty,
but nothing else was holding its own. The miles
bumped down everything that youth
zooms up. I thought: *Tart with dirty money,*
and kohl in her crow's-feet.

I loved to watch her being massaged. The no-nonsense Finn
fell on her like a mother bear, pounded her into
blubbering scarlet jellies.
Then, in the shower, a loofah's ape hand
rubbed her raw, wiped her clean of prints.
I did manic jumping-jacks
while she coiled wounded in black towels, Malevola
in her creepy-crawly robes.

We emerged from separate exits, pale and shriven.
She was swathed in Swakara lamb, her
other-woman lace rag crushed to her lips,
coughing, beset.
I put my hands in the pockets of my poorboy sweater
and walked thoughtfully home
through the cold, plum blue twilight.

43

How to Tell a Bird of Prey

Girls weighing less than a hundred pounds,
girls who look as though they were raised on
milk veal and summer wine,
can chew down through the roof
and devour whole families. This one wants

the man: rank and sexy as an old bobcat.
She likes his face, that mess of big prize vegetables
with rooty beard and spud chin, red onion cheeks
and hot toad tongue: *Wonderful things might happen,*
she reflects, *if I kiss a toad.*

She doesn't see his nose,
that crackbrain crackheart beak.
She doesn't mark his gaze,
beautiful blood in the raptor's eye.

Punch and Judy

Quick now, a match. (A rag flares
in a lump of grease.) The illumination's
crude, but still I see
your leotard, flung on a beam,
your mouth a slice of tangerine,
your clublike hand and arm
taking a whack at the cat—who's
cataleptic, and only sane
by fits and starts.
You can't stomach dinner.
You send me head over heels
with a mealy potato, flung in the eye—
how many years
since I first fell for you?—
and I paste you with a skillet
concealed in the net of a rusty bustle.
Hard words rattle like wheatberries
over the grinding surface of your teeth.
Your old grievance quivers,
renascent, evergreen:
your solitary pillow, Judy's weathered hide
denied. You seize it and shake it,
my ancient rump roast, your bone of contention,
and we rake it over the coals
once more.

Trial Separation

Our winter war progressed,
mounted on big guns.
Friends with a taste for hunting
pursued like borzoi,
knowing that if not here and now
then certainly at last,
the pale amazed head of one of us
would be lifted by its hair.
They counted casualties,
disqualified wild shots,
and gauged the foulness of the play.
They tested with jovial thumbs our fighting edges.
They discussed the lay of the land, and knew
whose native force would fail
in difficult terrain.
They sifted the situation
down to its last trace elements,
hoping to find two miniature and marbleized,
clinking pottery hearts—
for getting down to brass tacks
is a tradition of the tribe—

but warmer weather revealed us, amazingly, together:
not with new skin,
but with scars that would serve.
The borzoi were maddened,
they sprang after chamois and bags of anise,
they cooked up tales, and searched out enemy
camps to carry them to, and they pined:
until time, and their own
eager mettle, gave them a new
bloody hash to settle.

Hard Freeze for Lyn and Barry

Tonight. She lights the lights. The candle boggles
behind its hurricane shade.
Short of fire, short of rations, still, they've a cache of gamy
food for thought, enough to choke a horse.
The oak-hearted table groans beneath the hot potatoes
they slam down nightly, their prosecutors' frenzy to find
who has maimed/slain whom.
(After a hard night of home truths, like a Prohibition drunk,
she's blind for three days.)
His dogs glare from the corners and her *benjimana,*
weeping fig, stands naked, its green dream
shaken in the draft.
The coffee urn reflects their jawing faces and the details
of their mismatch: his surly bear's vest, her damnfool kimono.
Their jargon, stone-ground Chinook, hounds soft words to death.

Supper over, they prepare to get down to the nightly brass tacks—
to burnish guilt, and to call each other goat or bitch or boor—
but it's the coldest hour of the coldest month. Winter storms
through them. Her white breath can hardly support
these black-hearted names.

If they, sky-high, could fly their gooseflesh south—

but the wind chill, snowslide, icefall prepare to knock them cold.
If they're batted flat by a grizzly paw,
will friends dig them out by spring?

He never knew his place, any more than fire.
His hooded eyes, his prospector's beard
always hid the same old
new year's wishes, for gold, women, amazing strokes of luck,

while she mulled over a hundred flighty ways
of turning tail . . . and this year, too,
although she knows
they'll spend the winter cheek by jowl
munching their marriage, that seedy
apple of her eye, still, the numskull eel-blooded season
has, well within it, that old red coal:

let me fly, says a heart murmur,
let me fly by night.

The
Raptor's
Eye

Photographer

You've recorded every follicle
in the life of a peppercorn,
shot Mafiosos at play,
and your girlfriend
basks, swirled like a hoop
beneath a leopard-spotted lens,
her smile superimposed
on her high
starlet rump.

Here a voluptuous sculpture
swells in slow curves
its fabulous white hips,
pouts its breast
like a gigantic dove.
Modulations of the eye
reveal this to be a toilet
(though it could be genetic sister
to a trumpet lily.
One knows its scent is clean as a nun,
Immaculata.)

Your self-portrait
burns out the infrared film.
Having barely beaten the shutter speed,
you fix on the camera
a level necrotic gaze.
Coins of glass yellow as petals
shuttle you between themselves,
register you without comment:
your look of a lesser man-eater,
your old nautch eyes.

Fatemark

Whether you're the one darling of two pure people
forming a more perfect union
or just another evil strand in an evil head

months pump you through the Hotel Dream of the womb
(in which you'd lounged, sumptuously alone)
until time's up: you have the nerve,
you have the blood, and another red alien
rams through home country into outland
at a breakneck breakheart pace, now and ever
hothead first.

There are no orphans. Your fate,
the toughest mother you will ever know,
lifts you with heart lathering against her ribcage,
she stretches out her hand and claps it
to your crown, side and heel.
You're marked for life
with the good and ill of what you are.
Then with luscious lips,
with teeth filed into points
she cleats her mouth to your ear and breathes

you must live or else.

The Blackbird Bride

The porch smells of lime and white geranium
as May shows me her wedding album: "Black silk charmeuse . . .
my mother had died, and I'd never heard
Married in black, you'll wish yourself back."
The bride stands beatific full face, the groom's eyes say
See my cherie and the only buzzard luck evident that day
is a cement block mother-in-law in bobble fringe.
She gave them a bed sheet and a frying pan,
her doomy blessings whacked a young bride flat.

His mother moved in and rolled over them like The Blob.
The twins were born at seven months,
and although anyone could see they were premature,
the old woman made dirty jokes to her friends.
May was so mortified she almost died.
Her husband hated to come home, within a year
he became a bar philosopher: "I drink, therefore I am."
He grew ill and begged for giblets, chicken heart and feet
to help his liver, riddled to lace.
The smell of gut soup and the thought
He is incurable, and yet I am dying,
had May blacking out in closets like a crazy woman.
Then one day her mother-in-law the milk snake
ordered her to give blood to the blood bank. She said
"They need it, a mild winter fills the graveyard,
I've got my fifth gallon pin already."
May thought *Get away from me, old skull,*
"and although I was as weak as the twins, all the sudden
I'd had enough. I shouted NO,
pushed that big woman out the door,
kicked her fat can down the steps,
and threw her greasy cat after her."

Letty and the Sinister Synod

Letty's son Jim had wasted to wishbone and frog legs,
dying like a movie invalid in the heroic family bed.
The dark too was like a movie,
mercury-blue vapor of eucalyptus swirling to meet
icy angel faces at the glass.

Jim was the prom king at the funeral,
hair pomaded to a coronet.
The pastor said we must search and flay our hearts
for the tumor of sin,
confront our demons to disperse them.
For too long, he said,
certain people had caused God to feel disgusted,
displaying and disporting themselves,
drooling with carnal syrups.
Personally the pastor was stunned
at the great mercy of God
who instead of just saying *The hell with Jim,*
he had his fun, now he's got his,
had allowed Jim *to symbolically recapture purity*
through the grace of terrible suffering.

Letty concentrated on Jim's hair. She'd heard hair
stayed alive, filled coffins, covered the dead
with a horse blanket of eerily soft fur. She also knew
the dead were kept in the dark to retard spoilage.
Onions matured in the earth. The dead of her church
rose and rose: she pictured Jim
shining with dancing sweat,
yanked up like bait. She would never dare
touch his hair, turned to a mane of stars.
Just now Jim was smiling so gently,
enjoying God's sweet deal.

Burlesque Night at Le Cave

Bluebell lights sensitive as fingers
touch a breast or ear.
Here is the comic, a little old boll weevil
in a terry cloth tuxedo:
     Man: What's your ancestry, m'dear?
          Where were your folks from?
     Woman: I'm half Indian and half Scotch.
     Man: That's the way I like 'em, wild and tight.

Country girls full of yum-yum and apple pie
jump out of their pantalets
pursued by snake-oil salesmen, and we all
hoo-ha and spill our drinks. Here is the Blue Angel
with man-hungry fishnet legs swelling out her jackboots:
radium blond, mouthing
the great plums and hairy joints of German curse words.
She is wooed by clowns, clowns that oink, clowns that bray,
and pelted by fist-sized roses
out of which rabbits leap, and run away.
Ducks mill in the wings

and just then, ready or not, a splashy star
descends by rope and faces us, big dippers swirling:
it is La Violette:
and the audience breathes, *ma belle.*

Her cloak of chubby fox
purrs to the floor. Soon
her stockings of nude lilac
will have them jumping up and down

but just now she looks at us so quietly
with the bright eyes of the strongest cub.

Then the horns blow,
her hands white as bean flowers rise to her neck
and then above her head, her legs move
to the bandleader's passionate baton
and she looks into the dark room and says:

Whoever you are, here we go.

Cat-Burglar

He coasts home at midnight, brights dimmed,
back from some cutthroat high jinks.
His girl, Rapunzel in a trolley-red peignoir,
hangs out the window and waves the swag of hair
that she won at a carnival. She climbs on a chair
and, as it's a moonless night,
shoots her very own full moon.
Full of hopped-up whoopees, he races up the stairs,
and, made for each other, they embrace like mink.

Meanwhile, downstairs in the kitchen the landlady
nurses hot milk, eases the band on her sup hose
and wonders what's to be done
with the hood and his moll.
(She's had her doubts, ever since discovering
the magnum of Mumm's and the ten TVs, while the unattached
baby blue bidet seems to clinch matters.) They're
up to no good, and riding high on the swag.
But whether to call the police, or to raise the rent . . .

Now: there's music, and the second story man
and the carny queen are hoofing it
like a roomful of drunken Shakers,
rabid, hotfoot, Adventists whose time has come.
The landlady remembers suddenly *his* motorcycle vest,
with its pattern of nailheads,
and *her* push-up French bra, dangling from the line,
and seven multiflora bikini pants—white for Sunday,
blue for Monday, and so on to black lace for Saturday—
tonight is Saturday—

The landlady imagines them wallowing in mortal sin,
slick as hogs and hot as monkeys. She knows
it will end someday in a chute-the-chute down to hell

in ferocious primary colors—
and yet, as she turns out the light and climbs into her snuggies
(the darkness seems complete enough for an overnight growth
of mushrooms, or goiters)—
she tastes an instant's sad bile as she realizes
how entirely she is out of danger. No one will *ever*
get her from behind.

Swan Brother's Sister

*Then the girl led her brother home. She held him by the hand, and his
other hand and arm, which were still bewitched into a wing, he concealed
beneath a cloak. A neighbor came running out and said, "So, Karen, you
did save him after all!"*
*Karen looked into the eyes of her brother, which were dark, blank, and
wild, and said slowly, "Oh, well, save . . . Save is a big word."*

Modern addition to Hans Christian Andersen's "The Wild Swans"

Hard on the fingers, a cloak
made of thistles and yellow hair,
hard on the heart, your bleak glare

no memory of brother and sister
fleeing the reek of the death hut
and the witch a bag of bones in a red skirt
sneering at me *Little white dress, go away,*
hissing at you *I want you alive*
while your face went moony with dread and I thought
Mother was right, too handsome
for his own good.
I tried to save you, I always have.
I threw myself in between, and full in the face I took
the madwoman's horrible kiss, the boy's mad look.

She did take your life for a time.
It should have been me; I could have been
a swan for awhile and flown with witches
and called it fun.
But you never had the sand for flight.

At the beginning of our lives
you and I stood in the same folk painting:
blond boy with peach, dark girl with kitten.
Time passed, and one day

we stood in the same furnace.
Terror can slough a mind in a minute, but not mine.
I popped up a brawny journeycake woman,
tough as bark to the end of my days.

The cloak was hard
but I did it, I knitted
the thorns and curls, cloth of iron grew
from my bloody paw.
The witch was death,
but I beat her,
watched her guts pop out her mouth,
and brought you home.
Now you look like my brother,
and the neighbor calls you saved.
I keep meat on your bones, and at church
I parade you before the most powerful angel,
the one whose granite wings almost lift the roof.
I would try anything.
But day after day I see

that blank dilation in the eye
and beneath the breastbone, burnt caraway
where the star had been

and I know the furnace got you, furnace won,
and the swans' skein over the grey sea.
You live in the spell that is never broken,
too hot and cold for me.

Memory Jug

Stalking Joy

We began as greenbones barely
knowing to crawl: bumped against walls of the home cave
painted thick with ragemaster God, more hair
than a pack of wolves, and our own
perennially fruiting madonna whose sweet bell shape
was wrapped in lamb-smelling cardigans.

It was usually winter. The cold was a glittery grizzly,
with palisades of claws. We learned our place.
Northerners mate, ride, and die on glaciers,
where the bride's dress is an icefall of lace
and the corpse's full beard snows over his earth suit.
Red twilight turned to black frost

and the red brand of the home
saved as it burned. The hive of the family
provided abundance of sweet.
Still, the year came when I (mama's pearl,
papa's youth of flint) thought
canaries die here and plotted my own abduction.
Rock bricked me up,
front, back, top, and sides. Cave fire gilded
the coma of time. Never mind. The young,
like murder, like art, will out
in the most surprising places. And stubborn blood
melts rock.

Ross's Eyes

That week I'd storm down corridors in my mother's-milky
gauze robe, an angel's gown with a hot mammalian smell,
and stop short
at the nursery where you'd been called
"small: but not *too* small." There was a baby
web-footed like a cygnet, and piglet babies
with steel cords whipping from their pink trotters,
monitors clamped to chest and brain.
Space age Tom Thumbs blew out dolly cheeks,
sucked on petal tongues.
They looked about them with dark blue eyes
whose newborn fogginess
was daily dispelling. I'd spot you
and sit beside you, ticking with love, purple heart
on sleeve. Drakes of black curls
clung about your skull, elegant, elongate.

Crammed with butterfat, swilling fast and loose,
you'd look up. Forcemeat heart
on fire, my goosey stare
crossed yours. The starry eyeball
never faltered, looked back long and strong.
I was bulldogged by your eyes
and could only think weakly
of the Gene Vincent rocker:
Be Bop-a-Lula: he's
my baby now, my baby now, my baby now.

The Bad Review and My Sister

The serpent put its tongue in my ear
and hissed, "After you croak,
you will go to the red house
and meet Mr. Blaze
and in front of everyone
he will read aloud your poem,
the one where 'knees knees knees'
rhymes with 'please please please,'
and they will all puke."

"It is true, true," I gibber, "fall hammer strike,
forage fang, count my bones
and bury me where I fall—"

Then my sister stood up,
the one whose back is like a little wall
and whose children haul themselves up on her braids
hand over hand.
She nailed snake eyes with the black stare
that had driven Biblical escaped bulls
and demented hired hands to their knees,
and she said: "Snake, this woman is our beloved sister,
mother, daughter, aunt and niece, in whom
we are all well pleased. Furthermore
she was an infant prodigy, whose poems were
read at all the Reunions
from the age of five—"

(Lit-tle Star! sneered the serpent)
"—and as for you with your bad-tongue disease,
where I come from
people make wallets out of snakes."

The snake was visibly shaken.
He once more approached my ear, breathed
Catch you later,
and silently writhed away.

The Philosophy Major's Hair

Young men in that class grew fierce traditional snake-braids,
spearing the debate, others blackened the room
with enormous, spittle-shimmering Bolshevik
storm-beards of sedition.
While you called Nietzsche sentimental
and others roared you down,
I studied the earth-orb of your Jewish 'fro
and wished it were made for me.
Let it be mine,
your hard and stubborn head
with its yew-dense, mustang-brown fur of knots
tempting my hand. In it
I could have clipped topiary shapes of Adam and Eve,
their fast-breeding menagerie and garden of delight.
Then I would have said to you

Screw Nietzsche. Here's a mirror. See
how we could be.

Prodigal and Mother

The mother says:
There he goes, the little rat
born to break his mother's heart,
a black bottle mashed to his lips
and at his side a pink gaudy woman
dancing in her shift.
She leaps straight over a barrel
with her yellow marcelled hair
streaming back horizontally.
Downbound, and ripe for ruin,
who would ever guess
this man was once a breast-fed babe,
kissed my face, took fits,
was four times given up for lost,
and that as he began to plummet
oh God there goes my baby
I pounced for his curls
and braided him tight to earth
by the angel frizz of his head.
(Perhaps I should have let him fall.
At least he would have been
good and dead.)

The son says:
My mother the old grandiflora
will be deadheading roses
in her white garden, lilies croaking
to the tune of mortuary jewelry.
She expects me to roll in on my belly,
reeking of smut and junk.
What could I say to her?

The bogeyman came and took me away. Or perhaps,
Meet Rita, Mom. She's that nude over there,
combing her hair.
Mother would rise above the situation,
her oxfords on my neck,
and breathe perfect words from a painted saint.
She would offer tea, ear perked for my snivel:
I am guilty, guilty! Punish me!

In the dark, Rita turns to me
her jasmine pale
evening face. Her cool arms fall on mine
like fire. That life could have a mouth so soft
is what Mother feared,
in all her wildest dreams.

Fool for Love

All around me the high flyers plummet past.
The neighbor girl colors her grand fall
with severe strokes of black and white,
"Friday night I went out for cigarettes, met Chad;
Monday morning I woke up on Pine Island—
oh God, it's all a blank."
She draws on a cigarette, leaving me
to envious surmise.
Her irises range around, pure goofball
and yet marbled with lovely colors from the moon
and from Pine Island,
drugged lilac, blackest thorn.

I curse my little geisha feet
that never climbed a diving board.
Furiously I revise my script,
adjust for age and climate, determined that *someday*
I too shall have my splashy steamy plunge.

When I am an old burning loaf of a woman
(perhaps in Europe, where ripeness is all),
I will look into the eyes of some hairy attendant
who makes my bed, and counts my bones.
He will measure out my nitroglycerin,
give me little sips: "Are you comfortable?"
I'll ignore him, smell a rose. He'll say,
"What more can I do?" At last:
I'll give him a *film noir* look and hiss,
"Mon Dieu, are you not man enough to know?
Read my lips."

Rose's Farm

Rock-ribbed winter sunsets I would stop at Rose's farm,
where the rat-brown hump of the house
looked like a spawning place for felons
and sheep paddled in the black soup hole
of the barnyard. Rose herself had the face
of a purebred sheep, done up in challis,
and she never smiled. She had been driven from Poland
by some year so big and black that like an older,
white lace queen, she had not been amused,
then or ever. But she was glad to see me;
she swaddled me in afghans
smelling of all her favorite dogs
and rushed off for bulbous old-country bottles
that were bluish, and gritty, and kicked around,
as though they had known hard trouble and calamity.
This was Polish Bull's Blood, a red-black wine
that stuck to my tongue like the blade of a skate.
Rose sucked this busthead brew
calmly and sweetly, "real Galician mother's-milk,"
as she said: and she talked of Roy, her favorite,
the son who'd moved to Chicago
and was a hammer man at the stockyards.
One afternoon he appeared while I was there,
his arms full of fine caramellos, and whoopee cushions,
and records of the Goosetown Polka, and at last
Rose smiled. He asked after her heart,
that old red pumper: she struck her breast
with impatient contempt.
Then she cooked a big fat chicken
coughing with sweet paprika

and her remarks, like little dried black mushrooms,
expanded pungently in the red steam of the kitchen.
She set the platter before Roy,
and just then the loose kitchen door flapped open

and a little hog torn by a dog
ran in, its cascading chitlins
dragging on the floor.
Rose trapped him between her knees
and threw him on his side.
Then she stuffed the flowery pink wetness
of the guts back into their hole, looped them neatly,
and sewed up the screaming trotter
with needle and strong twine.
Roy sat with his fork in his hand, horribly green.
Finally he said: "Nature! Christ!"
And then: "Give me the kill floor
anytime."

Upon Learning My Enemy is Dead

I liked to think of that drunken fascist goat
down there in the gorilla-smelling dark,
lily dust on his heart
and not much meat on his bones.

His little toe circled the universe
on the charm bracelet of the constellations.
His hairspring
sprung, before mine.
I was left in possession,
the earth swelling with sugar
and flower spikes exploding
above a root monster so potent

but something was
coming around, coming around,

my last laugh without savor
(dust, ashes),
my blood denied its boil
(tears, lacerations),
the memory jug of the mind
robbed of its hottest jewel
(no one had such a bright eye as he!)

I missed his monster walk
I missed his monster talk

and I wished the earth could cough him up like Jonah,
that he could blast from the crypt with ZAP and POW,
raving and kicking like a comic book warrior

that I could feel again the life grip
of his villainous clutch.

Pheasant

His tawny heart thaws and turns,
hums with the season.

White water cracks ice.
Boulders wrench themselves
from the earth
like wintering mammoths,
black stone women in travail,
leaving wounds as long as dinosaurs.
Beside them, snowdrops blossom casually,
a perilous white essence.

The mood is one of hazard.
Every animal walks the earth,
his blank heart
and limited clear eye
absorbing the sun, observing
the conflict:
fox coat and pheasant talon,
a play of bronzes,
and later
wreaths of feathers, most beautiful,
articulated beak and copper claw.

Scarlet Fever

Look at Baby cried my sister at the door.

Night after night
my poor hot potato of a head
thrashed in sweats and dolors,
my green face, my red eyes fit to scare ghosts with.
I was prayed over by priests in chasubles,
and addled Mrs. Jessie, the neighbor lady
who liked me best,
secretly stuffed the bolster with
wolf's teeth, garlic bulbs, jack knives,
and clippings from the hired man's head, all to keep
poor baby from sailing away:
green hands clasping green lilies
to the breast of her little white nightie,
toes turned up.

Yes, I had the fungus-bungus, plague red.
It went ramping and raging over me
and kicked me live and burning
into the heady dark where once

hairy monkey hands
stuffed me in a sack, threw me over
to an oceanic roar. Blue ruin!
Thrown to the sea in a bag,
like my Golden Book Monte Cristo! *Oh Mama*
I cried from the toes up
and wriggled through the mouth of the sack
clean as a tadpole. Black bombers of fish
shot past my lips. A lush longhaired
mammal something floated blue belly up.
Undersea monsters reeled after
with hagfish screams and groans,

the gobs of their eyes
hanging out on sticks. *Mama*
I cried again. And a hand
wound itself in my hank of hair and lifted me.

Plucked from riptide: a blind snapped up and light
poured in, stone gold. My mother was combing
my lunatic mane. I looked like
several dwarfs at once, Grumpy, Sleepy, Dopey,
but my red ghoul face was gone. It was a mild
sweet potato pink, gummed with tears
like naive stars. *Duckie!* whooped Mrs. Jessie,
mashed me to her whopping bosom, and rushed off
in search of sugar pies and nourishing ham balls.
I sat up, looked outside: the sun was down.
A rose stood with its lips
pressed against the glass, archipelagos of leaves
flying into the dark.